Praise

"Betty Nadine Thomas's lovingly self-illustrated book of poems, *Unleashed*, takes the reader on a refreshingly profane and irreverent ride along the twists and turns of living life to the fullest. Thomas pulls no punches in this collection, and if you don't like it she'd say, 'go fuck yourself,' and does. That aside, she finds a delicious balance between beautiful profound moments and terrible torments, from which she always provides a retreat through new perspectives. 'Forget yesterday,' she writes, 'it's gone/ Look forward.' Digging into the memories of her history, she encourages us to look deeper into our own pasts, and inspires us to uncover the wisdom from there, helping us move with alertness, following 'the path back into the light.'"

—Buffy Aakaash, author of *Untangling the Knots*

"Betty Nadine Thomas's newest poetry chapbook, *Unleashed*, is exactly that! Brave, raw, and empowering, her poetry speaks the truth of who she is, and makes no apologies for having done so. Written in simple and direct language, Thomas's poetry collection ranges from poignant childhood memories, to earlier reflections of what it meant to be a lesbian in an unforgiving world, to thoughts on following her intuition, of lessons learned when we choose to ignore the voice within, and the darker and lighter sides of spirituality. Thomas's poetry is deeply introspective about herself, the world, and the journey taken to find her place within it. Through *Unleashed*, Thomas shows us there is freedom to be gained when we finally let go of the expectations of others, and grant ourselves permission to embrace who we are."

—Nicole Alyssa Gabert, poet and freelance book editor

"In *Unleashed*, Betty Nadine Thomas takes us along on her artistic, poetic, and sometimes comical journey to self-realization; from her Betty Wetty maidenhood to the tempered status of Betty Spaghetti, the aged crone develops resilience. She claims to still be 'fucked up, neurotic and insecure' but shares the wisdom and strength of purpose gathered along the way in her verses. 'Don't miss one second of it. Things change fast.' Betty echoes the pop culture of 80s icon Ferris Bueller, but she mourns the loss of the rebellious pot culture of the 60s. Betty Nadine Thomas covers a lot of ground...a lifetime indeed."

—Stephen Kastner, founder of Green Mountain Writers Group and media consultant at DesignWise Studios

UNLEASHED

UNLEASHED

POEMS AND DRAWINGS BY
BETTY NADINE THOMAS

Montpelier, VT

Unleashed copyright 2023 © Betty Nadine Thomas

Release Date: November 14, 2023

All Rights Reserved.

Printed in the USA.

Published by Rootstock Publishing
an imprint of Ziggy Media LLC
Montpelier, Vermont 05602

info@rootstockpublishing.com
www.rootstockpublishing.com

Softcover ISBN: 978-1-57869-154-8
eBook ISBN: 978-1-57869-155-5

Library of Congress Number:

Cover and interior art by Betty Nadine Thomas

Cover and interior book design by Eddie Vincent, ENC Graphics Services.

Author photo provided by author.

For permissions or to schedule a poetry reading, contact the author through her website www.bettynadinethomas.com.

To:
Helga Manning, Don Morang, Betsy Sweet,
Susan Thomas / Babb and Kathleen Morgan (1945-2022).
Love you all, my heart is huge because of you all.

Contents

You Want To Be What? 1

Oracle 3

FUCK, FUCK, FUCK. 5

Betty Spaghetti 7

Diddly 9

The Great Creator 11

Guide Me 13

Puppet On A String 15

Caged 17

LesBean Unleashed. 19

I Must 21

Mermaid Genes 23

Human 25

Those Were the Days 27

Cloud Feet 29

Dancing Trees 31

The Gift Around You 33

Passage 35

Acknowledgments 37

About the Author 39

You Want To Be What?

When I was small I wanted to be an artist.
When I grew up my parents said
You can't be an artist
You have to earn a living.

How stifling, toxic and debilitating.

Do you think they could think outside the box?
They couldn't.
Now I'm playing catch-up.

Don't have to earn a living
Not what it's all about
It comes from the soul
It's just got to get out.

At 70, I can safely say I'm an artist.
Screw you.
Still growing
Don't give a shit
About making a living.
Now I'm letting it all out.

Besides, if I hadn't had
All the life experiences
Wouldn't have a thing to write about.

Oracle

Ain't no fucking Oracle
Just an old Crone
Who's trying to unplug
her kitchen sink
Damn, hate it when my sink plugs.

Ain't no fucking Oracle
Just an old Crone
Trying to unplug her kitchen sink
Call a plumber
Hell no, it's my sink!
He ain't no Oracle either
Just got different tools
The old Crone succeeds
Without the boy plumber
Isn't life grand when you win one?

I ain't no fucking Oracle
Just a stubborn old Crone
Fixing her kitchen sink.

FUCK, FUCK, FUCK

Fuck, fuck, fuck
Kind of an offensive word
But so very much fun to say
Fuck, fuck, fuck
First learned the word as a small child
Can't remember where I heard it
One day, outside the kitchen window
About 4 years old, I started saying
Fuck, fuck, fuck
Loved saying it
Tickled my tongue and
Made the back of my throat vibrate
With the uck sound
My Mother happened to be in the kitchen
At the time, heard me saying
Fuck, fuck, fuck
Furiously, she came out the door and said
You are not to say that word
I looked at her and said, why not
it's fun to say
Fuck, fuck, fuck
You try it, I bet you'll like it too
Fuck, fuck, fuck
The aftermath
was not pretty.

Betty Spaghetti

Betty Spaghetti's my new nickname
It fits me just fine
When I was a kid
They called me Betty Wetty

I had to take this nasty medicine
It made me thirsty
So I drank lots of water
Yep, you know what happened
Betty Wetty
No wonder I'm fucked up
Neurotic and insecure

Some people even call me Betty Sweaty
We won't go into that

Betty Spaghetti suits me just fine
Bye, bye Betty Wetty
Now I'm just Betty Spaghetti
Still fucked up, neurotic and insecure
Still a little sane after all these years.

Diddly

As I get older, I realize most people
Are full of crap
They actually believe their own crap!
They pedal this stuff with absolute sincerity
Adamantly claiming their righteousness
Even indignant when called on their crap

News Flash

We're all full of crap
We know absolutely nothing
Nix, zero, zilch, nada, diddly, zip

We are just little gnats in the universe
Even *this* is completely full of crap.

The Great Creator

Where do those little dryer lint bunnies come from?
Seriously, I know they are in there
I put my wet clothes in the dryer
And in an hour there are tons of them.

Dryer lint bunnies are in there tumbling, tumbling around
Fornicating, making baby dryer lint bunnies
It's magical, amazing
Makes me feel like The Great Creator

But damn I get tired of cleaning up after the little fornicators
Wish they would move next door
Where I'm sure they came from
Then the neighbors can be The Great Creators
And I won't have to clean my dryer
Anymore.

Guide Me

In the early morning hours
The Spirits visit
Giving me guidance for the day
Sometimes the messages are profound
Sometimes funny
Sometimes down right crazy
Then I have to figure them out
They always guide my way

When I'm in a dark shadow place
They wait, I cannot find them
They stay away
Until I'm back in the light
Always patient with me
As I am just a humble being
Who doesn't always pay attention
To what they tell me
When I do I'm usually OK
When I don't, I stumble and bumble my way
Ridiculously making a mess of everything
They never anger, they wait until I awaken
To see things their way
In the early morning hours.

Puppet On A String

Am I just a puppet on a string
Bouncing up and down
Hitting the ground
With you pulling me
One way then the other, around and around
Not knowing which way to turn

Wondering to love you or not

Not knowing which way to turn
Around and around, one way then another
With you pulling me
Hitting the ground
Bouncing up and down
Am I just a puppet on a string

Caged

Caged
In a box of deception
Caged
In a box of manipulation
Caged
In a box of devastation
Caged
In a box of control
Caged
In a box of denial
Caged
In a box of annihilation
Caged
In a box of narcissism
Freed
To find reality
Freed
To find life
Freed
To see the lies
Freed
To find the light
Freed
To love again
Freed
To begin
Freed
To be ME.

LesBean Unleashed

Being a LesBean growing up was a curse
Deviant, deranged, disordered, obscenity
You can't be a LesBean
That's a perversion
You don't want to be a deviant pervert do you?
We hid, we didn't tell
We couldn't be whole
Oh shame, shame
Fuck, I just want to be me
I didn't do this to myself
I didn't chose it
It is who I am damnit
We fought just to be human
We're still fighting to just be
We were mentally ill, sick, unwanted
Unloved by our families and society
I just want to be me
Not hide the beautiful human inside
We were beaten, misunderstood
We suffered in silence
Families turned their backs
Said terrible things to the children
They were supposed to love
Leaving scars so deeply penetrating our insides
If your family can't love you who will
Tortured beyond belief
Good Christians turned away
Their hypocrisy running deep
Nope, you don't want to be a LesBean
Go hide the beauty inside
No more baby cakes
If you don't like who I am
Go fuck yourself
It's your problem not mine
I'm a fine LesBean
And now I'm UNLEASHED.

I Must

I love because I must
I teach because I must
I learn because I must
I grow because I must
I am generous because I must
I am compassionate because I must
I give because I must
I reveal myself because I must
I am peaceful because I must
I laugh because I must
I give because I must
I am kind because I must
I am gentle because I must
I am sensitive because I must
I am intuitive because I must
I am caring because I must
It is who I am because I must.

Mermaid Genes

Mermaid genes are in me.
They say, *you swim like a fish*.
You would too if you had Mermaid genes, swim in the sea and be free.
Mermaid genes are in me.
I've traveled the world in the water; seen everything in the sea.
A mythical creature, no, I can vouch
Mermaid genes are in me.
We swim because we must; it is our life, it is our soul.

Mermaid genes are in me.
Swimming, swimming free.

Human

Anger
Wasted energy
Rage
A cry for help
Hatred
Ignorance
Abuse
Control
Lying
Fear
Sadness
Momentary
Happiness
Striving
Ego
Laughable
Jealousy
Childish
Addiction
Everyone
Bigotry
Imbecilic
Killing
Insanity
Human
Infantile

Those Were the Days

Haight Ashbury, pot
Woodstock, pot
Vietnam protests, pot
San Francisco, pot
We were wild
We were free
We were rebellious
We thought we knew it all
Joan Baez, pot
Bob Dylan, pot
The Beatles, pot
The Rolling Stones, pot
Peter, Paul and Mary, pot
Simon and Garfunkel, pot
Judy Collins, pot
We were invincible
We were young, dumb
We were brave, pot
Now those free wild creatures
Are boring, middle-class establishment folk
What happened
They turned into their parents
They need pot
They lost themselves
Crumbled by society
No longer free
Mortgages, bills, kids, grandkids, rocking chairs
No Balls at all
Get off your asses hypocrites
Good shit you voted for *who*?
Accept the crap as it's served
It's well deserved
Pot, smoke more pot
Get it back together
Get to the crazy times

Get off your butts
Do something for someone
Besides yourselves
Get the crazy back
Try pot.

Cloud Feet

Walking on the clouds
Love my cloud feet

Soft and comfy
Bouncing on pillowy cushions

My cloud feet look like clouds
sky blue, pink and bouncy

Walking on cloud feet
way up high

Love my cloud feet
High in the sky

I can see everything
Way up high

Just bouncing on my cloud feet
Up in the air

Dancing Trees

Dancing trees outside my window
Sending tiny sparkling light
Shadows dancing on the walls
Frigid February cold chills my bones
With the ice illuminating my way
The sun peaks its head over the tops of the dancing, playing trees
Bringing the new day
Ending the shadows of the past
Clearer now, I see a new way, a beginning
That I never knew could happen
Bright with love, harmony and a peace I never thought possible
Leading me onward into a future, my destiny to find
Greater enlightenment profoundly filling me with gratitude for
What is to be
Chosen to follow a path
I know not where
I flow into it knowing
I am loved given gifts of gratitude to share.

The Gift Around You

Listen to the beautiful music
Look around you at the wonders that are in front of you

See the sky, the sun, the moon, the stars
Smile at the people

Find the peace in all the beauty around you
These are gifts from the Universe

Don't miss one second of it
Things change fast

Don't take these gifts for granted
Breathe the fresh air

Feel the water on your skin
Take it all in

Forget yesterday, it's gone
Look forward

Feel the beauty of the Universe
It's a Gift.

Passage

It's all about the journey as your life unfolds
One step then the next
Where will your path lead you
You will not know
Follow the light into the future
If it remains bright
You are on the right path
If it becomes dark
You have lost your way
Turn around look where you've been
Turn around look where you're going
Follow the path back into the light.

Acknowledgments

My sincerest humblest appreciation and gratitude to all of you who supported, counseled, kept me sane and safe during a most difficult life transition. Your continued support has made me a better, stronger, happier person than I could have ever imagined. This book has been a work of love, therapy, and a healing journey. As you have discovered I also have many Spirit Guides who counsel, scold, push and occasionally laugh at me but also keep me on my spiritual life path.

Even though this book is actually my second, it feels as though it is the first. It is a true representation of "who I actually am." It has also made me realize that I love creating. I'm not sure which part I actually love the best, the writing or the drawing. So I will continue to integrate both art forms as they are a part of me. In all actuality, I feel that I am only an instrument doing the work and the creations come from a place outside of myself.

I don't create to make money, there is no money writing poetry these days. I write to teach, open narrow negative minds and hopefully open hateful closed hearts. If only one person becomes a more loving human, recognizing that different religions, races and different sexual orientations does not make a person bad or evil but merely different, I will consider this work a raving success.

I could not have completed any of this without all of your love and support. Helga Manning, Don Morang, Betsy Sweet, my Sister Susan Thomas/Babb words just can't express how I really feel. You all are in my heart for eternity. Sadly, Kathleen Morgan passed while I was in the process of writing this. Kathleen Morgan was an absolute hero in her work assisting domestically abused women. She is deeply missed.

Thank you all. This one is for you guys, hope you enjoy it. Keep loving and laughing, life is too short to take any of it seriously.

This book would not be possible without Rootstock Publishing located in Montpelier, Vermont. Thank you for taking a chance on a 73-year-old poet, making a dream come true and giving me this opportunity. Samatha Kolber, owner of Rootstock Publishing, I am humbled not only by your wonderful poetry but by you as an outstanding human being and great work partner. Also, Eddie Vincent you were in my head when you created the wonderful cover, very much appreciate your fine work. To all those that contributed and helped make this chapbook come to life at Rootstock Publishing, love you all, thank you so very much for all your hard work, advice and excellency.

About the Author

Betty Nadine Thomas was born in California where she grew up and spent most of her life surfing in the ocean. Currently, she continues to boogie board and plans to be boogie boarding into her eighties, and more. Betty has traveled all over the United States working for the Red Cross, being deployed into many emergency disasters. Presently, and for the last ten years, she is an Emergency Management Agency Director in charge of emergency disasters in her local area.

Her passion for drawing and writing led her to create her first book of poetry *Purple Hats and Pink Tutus*. That passion continues and has been enhanced by her diversified life experiences and travels. These experiences have allowed her to meet and see many people, sometimes at the worst moments of their lives, which has allowed her to see and interact with humanity from a unique perspective. Some of these humanitarian perspectives are illustrated in her poetry and artwork.

Betty plans on continuing writing and drawing for the rest of her life. Her primary goal in her work is to teach, open negative narrow minds and open closed hateful hearts into accepting all people for whom and what they are regardless of race, religion and or sexual orientation.

Currently she lives in the smallest city in Maine.

 **More Poetry from Rootstock Publishing:**

Indigo Hours: Healing Haiku by Nancy Stone

Lifting Stones by Doug Stanfield

The Lost Grip by Eva Zimet

PoemCity Anthology: 2023 by Kellogg-Hubbard Library

Safe as Lightning by Scudder H. Parker

To the Man in the Red Suit by Christina Fulton

To learn about our Fiction, Nonfiction, and Children's titles, visit our website www.rootstockpublishing.com.

www.ingramcontent.com/pod-product-compliance
Lightning Source LLC
Chambersburg PA
CBHW020444090526
44586CB00045B/836